BEGINNING SIGN LANGUAGE SERIES

M000101314

An Alphabet of Animal Signs

by S. Harold Collins

Illustrated in part by Kathy Kifer and Dahna Solar

Special thanks to the Larson Family
for their help and knowledge.

Published by
Garlic Press
100 Hillview Lane #2
Eugene, OR 97401

ISBN 0-931993-65-2
Order No. GP-065

An Alphabet of Animal Signs is organized to present an animal sign for each letter of the alphabet. Standard animal signs are largely used; but for several letters of the alphabet common animal signs are difficult to identify. Thus animals such as jay, newt, ox or yak reflect an interpretation

We hope you will enjoy the beauty and language of this book. It is yet another addition to our Beginning Sign Language Series.

Alligator
Bear

Cat
(Stroke whiskers)
Dog
(Snap fingers and pat leg)
1
2

Frog
(Shows throat puffing)
Elephant

Giraffe
(Shows long neck)
Horse
(Show ear flapping)

Jay
(Make the letter J, then a bird beak.)
Insect
(The letter I on a crawling hand)

Kangaroo
Lion

Monkey
Newt

Parrot
Owl

Rabbit
Quail
2
1
(A bird beak,
then the letter Q)

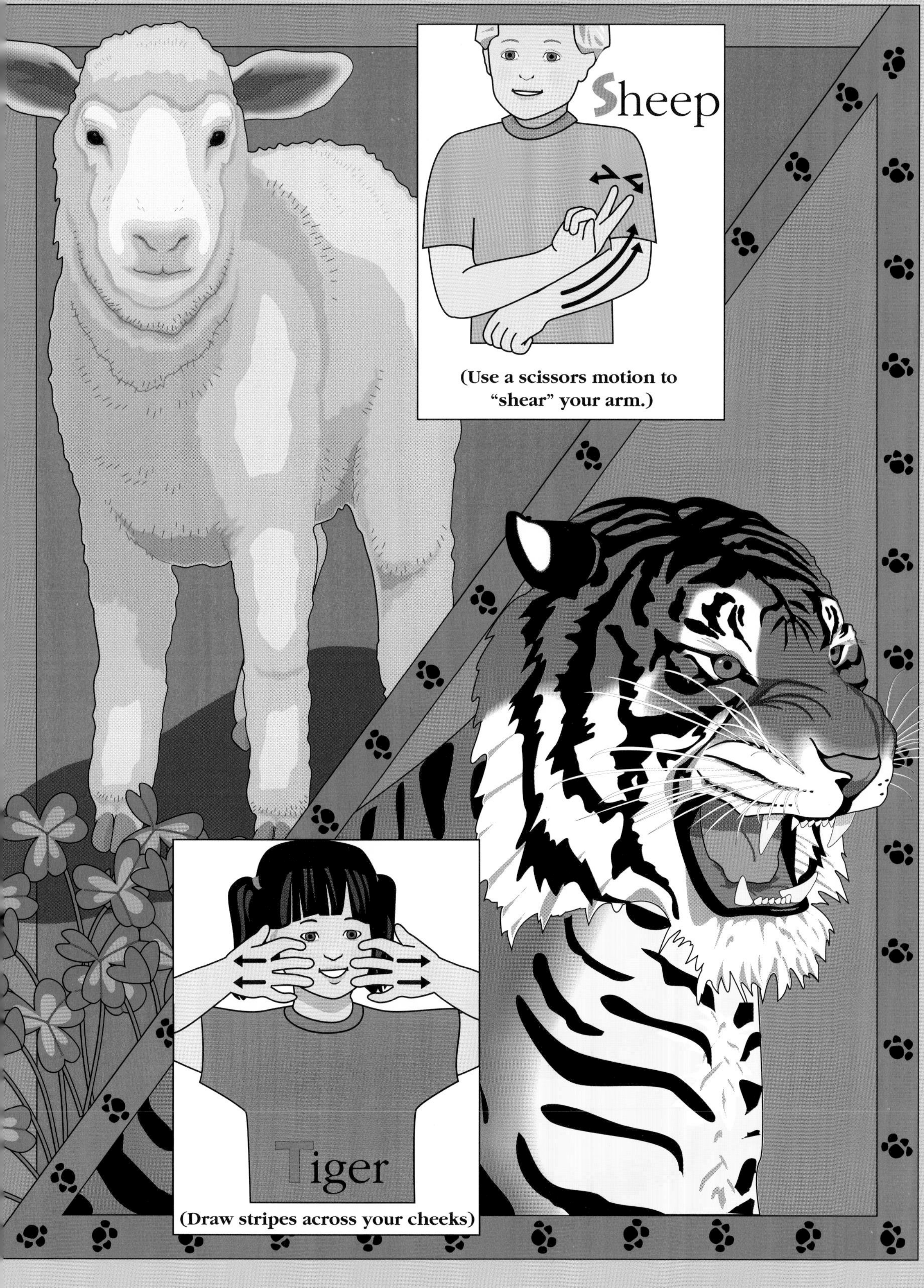
Sheep
(Use a scissors motion to "shear" your arm.)
Tiger
(Draw stripes across your cheeks)

Unicorn
Vulture

Wolf
(Stroke your long nose.)
OX
(The letters O and X)

Yak
(Use the letter
Y as a horn.)
1
2
Zebra